from SEA TO SHINING SEA
CONNECTICUT

By Dennis Brindell Fradin and Judith Bloom Fradin

CONSULTANTS

Freeman W. Meyer, Ph.D., Professor Emeritus of History, University of Connecticut

Robert L. Hillerich, Ph.D., Professor Emeritus, Bowling Green State University;
Consultant, Pinellas County Schools, Florida

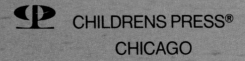

CHILDRENS PRESS®
CHICAGO

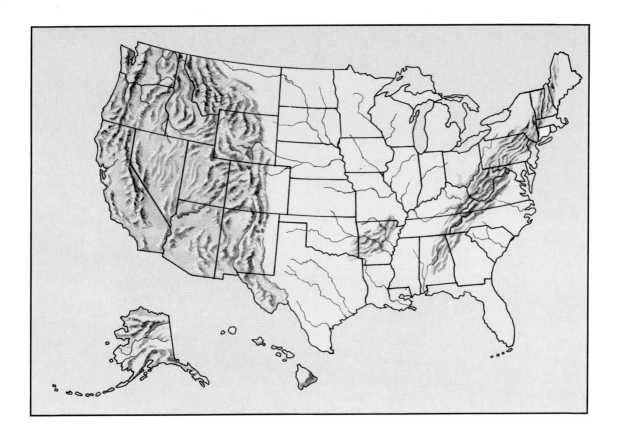

Connecticut is one of the six states in the region called New England. The other New England states are Maine, Massachusetts, New Hampshire, Rhode Island, and Vermont.

For our cousin Paul Brindel, with love

Front cover picture: Soldiers and Sailors Memorial Arch, Hartford; page 1: North Cove sunrise, Old Saybrook; back cover: Light House Point, New Haven

Project Editor: Joan Downing

Design Director: Karen Kohn

Typesetting: Graphic Connections, Inc.

Engraving: Liberty Photoengraving

Library of Congress Cataloging-in-Publication Data

Fradin, Dennis B.
    Connecticut / by Dennis Brindell Fradin & Judith Bloom
Fradin.
      p.   cm.—(From sea to shining sea)
    Includes index.
    ISBN 0-516-03807-9 (lib. bdg.) ISBN 0-516-26124-X (pbk.)
      1. Connecticut—Juvenile literature. [1. Connecticut.] I.
Fradin, Judith Bloom. II. Title. III. Series: Fradin, Dennis B. From
sea to shining sea.
F92.3.F72 1997   93–44696
974.6—dc20   CIP
                                                               AC

Table of Contents

Sledding on Johnnycake Hill, Old Lyme

Introducing the Constitution State

Connecticut is located in the northeastern United States. Its name comes from the Indian word *quinnehtukqut*. That means "beside the long river." The Connecticut River runs through the whole state.

Connecticut was one of the thirteen colonies. Colonial leaders drew up the first written constitution in the Americas. It was called the Fundamental Orders of Connecticut. Later, Connecticut became one of the thirteen original states. Connecticut people helped frame the United States Constitution. Connecticut is nicknamed the "Constitution State."

In colonial times, Connecticut became a manufacturing center. Today, the state is still an important leader in industry. Helicopters and computers are made there. Hartford, the state capital, is an insurance center.

Connecticut is special in other ways. Where is Yale University? Where do the Whalers play hockey? Where was Dr. Benjamin Spock born? The answer to these questions is: Connecticut!

A picture map
of Connecticut

*Overleaf: A pond in
autumn, Whittemore
Glen State Park*

From Mountains to Seacoast

From Mountains to Seacoast

Connecticut is the farthest south of the six New England states. Rhode Island is Connecticut's neighbor to the east. Massachusetts lies to the north. New York is to the west. Long Island Sound splashes against southern Connecticut.

Boulders at Stonington

Connecticut has 5,018 square miles of land. Its land is covered with mountains, valleys, and seacoast. The Taconic Mountains are in northwest Connecticut. Mount Frissell stands there. It is the state's highest point. Connecticut's part of Mount Frissell rises 2,380 feet above sea level. The Central Valley runs north to south. It is in the middle of the state. The valley was formed by the Connecticut River. Connecticut's seacoast is 618 miles long. Important towns lie along the coast.

Rivers and Lakes

The Connecticut River begins in northern New Hampshire. It flows southward for 407 miles. The river divides Connecticut almost in half. The Connecticut ends its journey by emptying into

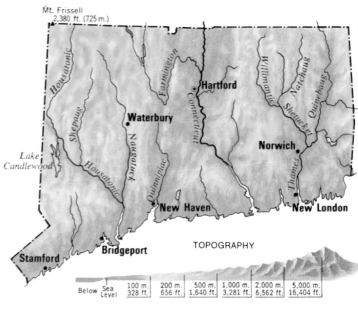

TOPOGRAPHY

	Below Sea Level	100 m. 328 ft.	200 m. 656 ft.	500 m. 1,640 ft.	1,000 m. 3,281 ft.	2,000 m. 6,562 ft.	5,000 m. 16,404 ft.

Long Island Sound. The state's other rivers include the Housatonic, the Naugatuck, and the Quinnipiac.

Left: Kent Falls State Park in western Connecticut

Connecticut has about 6,000 lakes and ponds. Most are small. Lake Candlewood is Connecticut's largest lake. It covers about 10 square miles in western Connecticut.

WOODS AND WILDLIFE

Nearly two-thirds of Connecticut is covered with forest. The white oak is the state tree. Maples, pines, hemlocks, hickories, and birches also grow there.

Beaver

Great blue heron

The mountain laurel is the state flower. This woodland plant has white and pink blossoms.

White-tailed deer live in Connecticut's woods. Beavers, river otters, and muskrats are found along the rivers and streams. In the winter, harbor seals sun themselves on rocks along the coast.

The robin is the state bird. Great blue herons catch fish in Connecticut's waters. Bass, perch, and trout swim in the streams. Cod, swordfish, lobsters, oysters, and clams are found along the coast.

CLIMATE

Connecticut has a mild climate. Many summer days see temperatures of about 80 degrees Fahrenheit.

On most winter days, the temperature climbs near 40 degrees Fahrenheit. At times, though, the state can get very hot or very cold.

"Northeasters" sometimes strike Connecticut. These windstorms come from the northeast. Northeasters also produce heavy rains. In the winter, they can also dump a lot of snow. Over 20 inches of rain fall on the state each year. From 10 to 25 inches of snow cover parts of the state.

Now and then, hurricanes hit the coast. These giant storms blow in from the ocean. The "New England Hurricane" of 1938 killed eighty-five Connecticut people.

Ducks swimming in a Middletown pond after a snowfall

11

From Ancient Times Until Today

FROM ANCIENT TIMES UNTIL TODAY

More than 100 million years ago, dinosaurs roamed across Connecticut. Their footprints have been found near Rocky Hill. The dinosaurs died out before there were people living on earth.

About 2 million years ago, the Ice Age began. Glaciers covered all of Connecticut. These slowly moving sheets of ice scooped out holes in the ground. When the ice melted, the holes became lakes. The Ice Age ended about 10,000 years ago.

Opposite: A Connecticut Farmyard in Winter is one of artist George Henry Durrie's many paintings of Connecticut scenes.

AMERICAN INDIANS

As the Ice Age was ending, people reached Connecticut. Over time, they formed separate groups. By the 1600s, Connecticut had about sixteen groups, or tribes. They included the Pequot, Tunxis, Quinnipiac, and Podunk Indians.

The Indians lived in villages near rivers and the coast. Their homes were built with wood and bark. The women grew potatoes, pumpkins, corn, squash, and beans. The men hunted deer and bears. They caught fish in the rivers and coastal waters.

Children exploring the Grass House at the Institute for American Indian Studies in the town of Washington

13

The people of the Netherlands are called Dutch.

Adriaen Block was an explorer from the Netherlands. He was the first European known to come to Connecticut. Block arrived in 1614. He and his group sailed up the Connecticut River. They were met by friendly Indians at present-day Hartford.

The Netherlands claimed Connecticut. In 1633, the Dutch built a small fort at Hartford. The Dutch traded for furs with the Indians. In exchange, the Indians received guns and kettles. The Dutch built no towns in Connecticut.

Also in the 1630s, English colonists arrived in Connecticut. They came from Massachusetts. These people found good farmland in the Connecticut River valley. Soon, the English colonists built towns. They founded Windsor in 1633. Wethersfield was settled in 1634. Hartford was begun in 1635. These three towns stood close together on the Connecticut River. In 1636, they joined together as the Connecticut Colony.

Hartford was named for Hertford, England.

New Haven Colony was founded in 1638. It was on the coast. By 1643, New Haven Colony had five towns: New Haven, Milford, Guilford, Stamford, and Branford.

Many Indians were friendly with the settlers. They taught the settlers to grow corn and other crops. But the Pequots didn't want the settlers on their land. The Pequots were Connecticut's largest tribe. In 1636, a settler was killed. The colonists blamed the Pequots. This led to the Pequot War (1636-1637). The colonists burned a Pequot village. It was near what is now West Mystic. More than 700 Pequot men, women, and children died. The Pequots were defeated.

More than 700 Pequot Indians were killed in the Pequot War.

A statue of the Reverend Thomas Hooker

Government in Colonial Connecticut

Reverend Thomas Hooker arrived in Hartford in 1636. He became a leader of the Connecticut Colony. Hooker believed in the Puritan religion. Puritan leaders chose government leaders. But Hooker felt that the people should elect their own leaders. In 1639, the Connecticut Colony approved the Fundamental Orders. This set of laws was based on Hooker's ideas. But only men who acted like Puritans could vote. The Fundamental Orders was the first written constitution in the Americas.

In 1662, the king of England gave Connecticut Colony a charter. The charter allowed the colonists more control of their government. It also gave Connecticut Colony all the land in present-day Connecticut. This included New Haven Colony.

In 1685, a new king ruled England. He wanted more control over the American colonies. In 1686, the king united Connecticut with nearby colonies. The new colony was called the Dominion of New England. The colonists had less say in their government than before.

Sir Edmund Andros was the dominion's governor. On October 31, 1687, Andros demanded Connecticut's charter. Connecticut's leaders hid the charter in a hollow oak tree. This tree was called the Charter Oak. It came to stand for Connecticut's love of freedom.

Even without the charter, Andros seized Connecticut. But the dominion didn't last long. The king was overthrown in 1688. In 1689, the colonists got rid of Andros. Connecticut was a separate colony again.

A Successful Colony

Connecticut was one of the most successful of the English colonies. By 1700, almost 26,000 people

The white oak was named the state tree because of the importance of the Charter Oak (below).

lived there. Only Massachusetts, Virginia, and Maryland had more people. Connecticut farmers grew corn, wheat, and tobacco. Fishermen brought back tons of fish from Long Island Sound. Farther out in the Atlantic, they hunted whales.

Education was important to the colonists. In 1650, Connecticut passed a law. Each town of fifty people had to pay for a school. In 1702, Yale College opened. Now it is Yale University.

Connecticut became a great manufacturing center. By the 1730s, Connecticut hats were famous in England. Simsbury was known for copper. Salisbury factories made iron goods. New London became a shipbuilding center. In 1740, Edward and William Pattison of Berlin made the first American tinware. This included plates, cups, saucers, and other household goods.

Connecticut Yankee peddlers packed tinware, buttons, and cloth into carts. They traveled about selling their wares. People joked that these peddlers sold small pieces of wood as nutmegs. Nutmeg is a spice. As a result, Connecticut came to be called the "Nutmeg State."

The *Connecticut Courant* began in 1764. Today its name is the *Hartford Courant*. It has been published longer than any other American newspaper.

This iron furnace in East Canaan was used by early iron forgers.

The nickname "Yankee" for a New Englander may have come from Jan Kees *(John Cheese), a Dutch nickname for Connecticut's English settlers.*

Connecticut played an important part in the French and Indian War (1754-1763). In that war, England and France fought for control of North America. Many Indians fought for France. The colonists helped England. No fighting took place in Connecticut. Yet, Connecticut sent about 5,000 soldiers to help the English. England won the war.

THE REVOLUTIONARY WAR

The French and Indian War cost England much money. To raise funds, England taxed the American

This Yankee peddler had his cart crammed with wares to sell on his travels.

colonists. The colonists hated those taxes. In 1775, fighting started in Massachusetts between England and the colonies. Soon, 3,600 Connecticut men marched to Massachusetts to help. They fought at the Battle of Bunker Hill in Boston. Connecticut general Israel Putnam told the Americans: "Don't fire until you see the whites of their eyes."

These early battles marked the beginning of the Revolutionary War (1775-1783). In 1776, the colonies declared themselves independent of England. They called themselves the United States of America. About 41,000 Connecticut troops fought for America's freedom.

During the war, Jonathan Trumbull was Connecticut's governor (1769-1784). He sent food, guns, and ships from Connecticut to help win the war. George Washington nicknamed Connecticut the "Provisions State." He called Trumbull "Brother Jonathan." For a time, people called the United States "Brother Jonathan."

The British raided Connecticut's coastal towns. Hundreds of Connecticut people died in those raids. Connecticut's greatest losses took place at New London and Groton. The Battle of Yorktown in Virginia was the war's last battle. With the victory there, the United States won its freedom.

Connecticut Governor Jonathan Trumbull ("Brother Jonathan")

THE FIFTH STATE

In 1787, American leaders wrote the United States Constitution. This was a new framework for the country's government. But the men argued over this point: How many lawmakers would each state send to Congress? Roger Sherman of Connecticut helped settle this problem. He came up with the Connecticut Compromise. Each state would have two lawmakers in the Senate. But states with more people would send more lawmakers to the House of Representatives.

Eli Whitney (above) invented the cotton gin (below) in 1793.

Connecticut approved the Constitution on January 9, 1788. That day it became the fifth state. Connecticut became known as the "Constitution State."

The new state became a center for invention. In 1793, Yale graduate Eli Whitney invented the cotton gin. This machine removed seeds from raw cotton. The cotton gin helped cotton become a giant crop in the South. Connecticut's first cotton mill was built in 1794. Raw cotton was turned into cotton cloth at the mill.

In 1808, in Plymouth, Eli Terry was the first to make large numbers of clocks. Seth Thomas opened a clock shop in 1812. It became the world's largest clock factory. In 1839, in Naugatuck, Charles Goodyear found a way to strengthen rubber. His process was called vulcanization. It helped rubber withstand heat and cold. Samuel Colt of Hartford invented the repeating pistol in the 1830s. Linus Yale of Stamford invented the modern lock in 1848.

Two Connecticut dentists found ways to take the pain out of operations. In 1845, Hartford dentist Horace Wells showed how nitrous oxide put patients to sleep. Farmington dentist William Morton did this with ether in 1846. When these drugs are used, patients feel no pain.

During the state's early years, many Connecticut people moved west. No state did more to settle the United States than Connecticut. Many Connecticut people moved to New York and Vermont. Others settled Ohio, Wisconsin, Michigan, and Minnesota. By 1831, Connecticut had only one-fiftieth of the country's people. Yet, one-third of United States senators had been born there!

Thousands of Connecticut people moved west to settle in other parts of the United States.

THE CIVIL WAR

When Connecticut was a colony, many of its rich families owned slaves. After 1784, Connecticut slaves received their freedom when they turned twenty-five. Connecticut's last slaves were freed in 1848. Slavery was no longer allowed in the other northern states. In the South, though, slavery continued. Black slaves grew cotton and other crops.

Many Connecticut people fought slavery. Harriet Beecher Stowe did so with her pen. Her book *Uncle Tom's Cabin* turned many people against slavery. Some Connecticut people helped southern slaves who were escaping to Canada. They turned their homes into hiding places.

Slavery and other matters led to war between the North (the Union) and the South (the Confederacy). This was called the Civil War (1861-

Union soldiers gather with their families in Connecticut.

1865). Connecticut sent more than 57,000 troops to fight for the North. They included 2,000 black soldiers. Connecticut's factories sent rubber boots, wagons, guns, and gunpowder. In 1865, the war ended and the southern slaves were freed.

INDUSTRIES, WARS, AND DEPRESSION

Hartford became the country's insurance center in the late 1800s. The first United States accident insurance company began in Hartford in 1863. The first United States auto insurance was issued in Hartford in 1898.

Manufacturing was also booming in the state. By 1900, most of the country's bells were made in Connecticut. Guns, bullets, hats, cloth, and typewriters were also made there. People from Europe and Canada came to work in Connecticut factories. By 1910, the state's population topped 1 million.

In 1910, the United States Coast Guard Academy was established. It is in New London. People train there to become Coast Guard officers. In 1917, the navy opened the United States Naval Submarine Base. It is at Groton.

That same year, the country entered World War I (1914-1918). Nearly 70,000 Connecticut people

This picture of a cotton mill in Taftville was taken about 1913.

The Coast Guard protects United States coastal waters and rescues people at sea.

25

helped win the war. Connecticut's factories turned out uniforms, guns, and bullets.

The Great Depression hit the country in 1929. This time of widespread hardship lasted ten years. By 1932, one-fourth of the state's workers were jobless. Wilbur Cross was Connecticut's governor (1931-1939). He signed laws that helped the elderly and the unemployed.

World War II (1939-1945) helped end the depression. The United States entered World War II in 1941. Connecticut's goods helped win the war. About seventy-five submarines were built at Groton. United States forces flew in airplanes with Connecticut-made engines. The state sent 233,000 men and women to war.

POPULATION GROWTH, PROBLEMS, AND SOLUTIONS

Between 1950 and 1970, Connecticut gained more than 1 million people. This was its biggest twenty-year gain ever. Many newcomers with money settled in the suburbs. At the same time, many wealthy people left Connecticut's big cities. They, too, settled in the suburbs. Hartford, Bridgeport, and New Haven became some of the country's poorest cities.

Wilbur Cross was one of the oldest governors any state has had. He served until he was seventy-seven years old.

During World War II, workers at the Colt Arms Factory in Hartford made machine guns and other weapons.

26

In the 1980s and 1990s, many companies left Connecticut. Thousands of the state's people lost their jobs. Many of those people lived in the cities.

Connecticut leaders have tried to help the cities. The state adopted a new constitution in 1965. It gives the big cities more voting power. In 1979, Connecticut set up a new school-funding system. More state money reaches schools in poor areas.

Lowell P. Weicker, Jr., became governor in 1991. That year, he began the state's first income tax. Voters were very angry with the governor for giving them more taxes. In 1994, Governor Weicker did not seek reelection and John Rowland became the new governor.

The Lutz Children's Museum, in Manchester

Overleaf: A costumed cyclist on a high-wheeler tricycle at Mystic Seaport

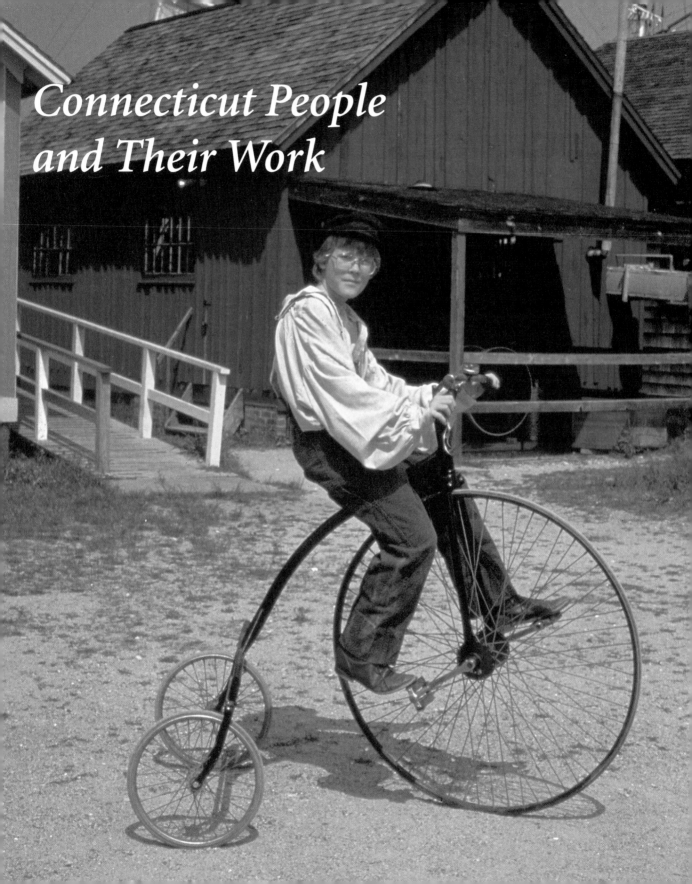

Connecticut People and Their Work

Connecticut People and Their Work

Connecticut's nearly 3.3 million people make it larger than twenty-three other states. Of the six New England states, only Massachusetts has more people.

About 87 of every 100 Connecticut people are white. Their ancestors came from such places as England, Italy, Ireland, Poland, France, and Canada.

Nearly 300,000 Connecticut people are African-Americans. About 220,000 of the state's people are Hispanic. Their families came from Puerto Rico, Mexico, and other Spanish-speaking lands. Lately, people from Asia have been Connecticut's fastest-growing group. They number over 50,000. Connecticut is also home to about 7,000 American Indians.

About 8 percent of Connecticut people are black and about 6.5 percent are Hispanic.

Connecticut ties for first place with Massachusetts in percentage of college graduates. About 27 percent of Connecticut's adults are college graduates. A good education helps them get good jobs. The average Connecticut resident earns more than $28,000 a year. This is the country's highest per-person income.

Connecticut People at Work

More than one-half of the state's people have jobs. About 575,000 of Connecticut's 1.7 million workers provide services. They include insurance workers, doctors, and car repairers. Connecticut is headquarters to 150 insurance companies. There are fifty-five companies in the Hartford area. They include several of the country's biggest life insurance companies.

About 360,000 Connecticut workers make products. Transportation equipment leads the list. This includes helicopters, submarines, jet engines, and car parts. Computers and other machinery are also made in Connecticut. So are medical instruments, watches, and clocks.

Left: A telephone technician
Right: A Hartford firefighter

Almost 400,000 Connecticut people sell goods. Two food-store chains are based in Windsor Locks. More than 200,000 Connecticut people work for the government. Among them are teachers, police officers, and the governor.

Farming employs more than 20,000 Connecticut people. The state is a leading grower of flowers and shrubs. Connecticut chickens produce about 1 billion eggs a year. The state's cows produce about 500 million pounds of milk yearly. Apples, pears, beef, hay, mushrooms, and tobacco are other farm goods.

More than 1,000 Connecticut workers are miners. They pull crushed stone, sand and gravel, and clay from the ground. About 1,000 earn their livings by fishing. Clams, oysters, lobsters, scallops, flounder, and shad are the main catches.

Connecticut is a leading grower of flowers. These pansies are being grown in Durham.

In New England, only Maine produces more eggs than Connecticut. Only Vermont and Maine produce more milk.

Overleaf: Mystic Seaport

A Trip Through the Constitution State

A Trip Through the Constitution State

Connecticut offers much to see and do in a small area. The state has big cities and beautiful countryside. Many historic sites add to Connecticut's charm.

The Coast

Long ago, taverns provided food and a place to spend the night.

Downtown Stamford: Glass buildings at dusk

Greenwich is at the state's southwest corner. It is a good place to start a coastal tour. In 1779, General Israel Putnam was staying at Knapp Tavern in Greenwich. The British approached. Although Putnam was sixty-one years old and overweight, he escaped. "Old Put" rode his horse down a steep cliff. The tavern is now called Putnam Cottage in his honor.

Stamford is east of Greenwich along the coast. With about 106,000 people, it is the state's fifth-biggest city. Stamford is known for the many large companies based there. They include Xerox and Waldenbooks. Stamford's Bartlett Arboretum has flowers and trees from around the world.

Farther along the coast is Norwalk. There stands Lockwood-Mathews Mansion. It has fifty

rooms. People call it a palace. The Maritime Center is another highlight of Norwalk. Sharks and harbor seals from Long Island Sound can be seen there. The center also has displays on Connecticut's seafaring history.

Bridgeport is a short way up the coast from Norwalk. It was settled in 1639. Today, Bridgeport has almost 142,000 people. It is the state's biggest city.

Phineas T. Barnum lived in Bridgeport in the 1800s. He ran "The Greatest Show on Earth," a famous circus. Bridgeport's Barnum Museum was built with money left in his will. A talking statue of

A view of Bridgeport

Feeding the seals at the Maritime Center in Norwalk

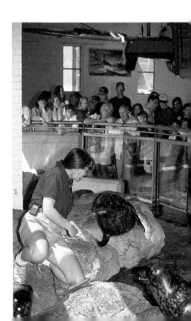

The P.T. Barnum Museum in Bridgeport

Branford College at Yale University, in New Haven

Barnum greets visitors. Items relating to Barnum are displayed. They include General Tom Thumb's little carriage. Thumb was from Bridgeport. He was about 2.5 feet tall. Thumb was part of Barnum's circus.

Because of its lovely parks, Bridgeport is called the "Park City." Barnum donated land for Washington and Seaside parks. Bridgeport also has the state's biggest zoo. Beardsley Zoo is known for its Siberian tigers. Bridgeport's Discovery Museum is a good place to learn about space travel.

New Haven is midway along the coast. With more than 130,000 people, it is the state's third-

biggest city. Yale University is at New Haven. Yale runs the Peabody Museum of Natural History. Dinosaur fossils are among its treasures. The Yale University Art Gallery was founded in 1832. It is the country's oldest college art gallery.

The Shore Line Trolley Museum is near New Haven. About 100 old trolley cars can be seen there. Trolley rides are offered every thirty minutes.

The Thimble Islands are not far from New Haven. Captain Kidd, a pirate, reportedly hid treasures on Money and Pot islands.

Guilford is not far from New Haven. Connecticut's oldest home is there. The Henry Whitfield House was built in 1639. It is also New England's oldest stone building.

Monte Cristo is a famous New London landmark. It was Eugene O'Neill's boyhood home. O'Neill became a great playwright. His play *Long Day's Journey Into Night* is set in Monte Cristo. Today, the home is open to visitors.

The United States Naval Submarine Base is at Groton. That is across the Thames River from New London. The base is home port to many submarines. In 1954, the *Nautilus* was launched from Groton. It had also been built there. The *Nautilus* was the first nuclear submarine. Today, visitors can

The Trolley Museum in East Haven

Frank Sprague of Milford, Connecticut, helped invent the trolley in 1888.

The main boat shop in Mystic Seaport

board the famous sub. It is called the USS *Nautilus* Memorial.

Mystic is near the state's southeast corner. Fast clipper ships were built there during the 1800s. Mystic was also a whaling port. Mystic Seaport is a popular spot in Mystic. It includes many homes and shops of the 1800s. There are also more than 400 sailing vessels. Visitors can explore the *Charles W. Morgan*. Built in 1841, it is the country's last wooden whaling ship.

THE EASTERN INTERIOR

Connecticut's eastern region has no big cities. It does have many pretty farms and small towns. Uncasville is in southeastern Connecticut. It was named for the Mohegan leader, Chief Uncas. He sided with the settlers during the Pequot War. The Tantaquidgeon Indian Museum is at nearby Montville. Uncas's family founded the museum. Mohegan baskets and dolls can be seen there.

Norwich is to the northeast. It has a monument to Uncas. He gave land for the town. Norwich is also the site of Leffingwell Inn. American leaders met there during the Revolutionary War.

The Gillette Castle in Hadlyme

William Gillette was a descendant of Thomas Hooker.

Hadlyme is southwest of Uncasville. Twenty-four-room Gillette Castle stands on a hill there. William Gillette spent five years and $1 million building the house. Gillette was a stage actor known for playing Sherlock Holmes.

Moodus is a few miles north of Gillette Castle. Rumbling noises come from beneath the town. Underground rock movement causes these "Moodus Noises." An earthquake shook the town in 1791. But one story says that witches cause the noises. They are said to be fighting in a cave at nearby Mount Tom. Another story says that the Devil is playing his violin atop nearby Chapman Falls. Meanwhile, witches below brew magic potions. The waterfall is now part of Devil's Hopyard State Park.

Northeast of Moodus is Lebanon. Jonathan Trumbull was born and lived there (1710-1785). Governor Jonathan Trumbull House has a secret room with a high window. Trumbull could work there without fear of being shot by the British. The Revolutionary War Office is also in Lebanon. This was where "Brother Jonathan" led the war effort.

Willimantic is a short ride north of Lebanon. The Windham Textile and History Museum is there. It tells about the life of Connecticut factory workers during the 1800s. The University of Connecticut is farther north at Storrs. With about 26,000 students, it is the state's biggest school.

Coventry is southwest of Storrs. Nathan Hale was born there. He was an American spy during the Revolutionary War. The Nathan Hale Homestead was his family's home. Hale's Bible and army trunk can be seen at the homestead.

The Nathan Hale Homestead, in Coventry

TOWNS IN THE CONNECTICUT RIVER VALLEY

Hartford lies on the Connecticut River's west bank. Nearly 140,000 people live there. It is the state's

The state capitol, in Hartford

second-biggest city. Hartford is known as the "Insurance Capital of the World." It is also the capital of Connecticut.

Long ago, Connecticut lawmakers met in Hartford's Old State House. It was completed in 1796. Today's lawmakers meet in the golden-domed state capitol. A carving of the Charter Oak is on the building. The real tree was destroyed in a storm in 1856. The Soldiers and Sailors Memorial Arch is near the capitol. It honors Hartford's Civil War troops.

The Mark Twain Mansion

The New England Air Museum, in Windsor Locks

The Mark Twain Mansion stands in Hartford. Twain wrote *Tom Sawyer* and *Huckleberry Finn* in the house. The Harriet Beecher Stowe House is next door. Stowe moved there after she wrote *Uncle Tom's Cabin*.

Hartford has the country's oldest public art museum. The Wadsworth Atheneum was founded in 1842. The Museum of Connecticut History houses the 1662 charter that was hidden in the Charter Oak. Hartford also has a National Hockey League team. Its name is the Hartford Whalers.

Windsor is Connecticut's oldest town. It is north of Hartford. Oliver Ellsworth's birthplace is at Windsor. Ellsworth was the country's third chief

justice (1796-1800). The New England Air Museum is at nearby Windsor Locks. Visitors can see nearly 100 aircraft. The oldest airplane there is from 1909.

Farther north is East Granby. The Old New-Gate Prison and Copper Mine is there. In 1707, it was one of the country's first copper mines. The mine was turned into a prison in 1773. Stairs lead down into the old mine and prison. Visitors can explore the dark tunnels.

Old New-Gate Prison and Copper Mine

Wethersfield, Rocky Hill, and New Britain are south of Hartford. The Joseph Webb House is in the center of Wethersfield. George Washington planned the Battle of Yorktown there. Dinosaur State Park is at Rocky Hill. Nearly 200 million years ago, 24-foot-long dinosaurs made tracks there. Today, visitors can make plaster casts of the footprints. The Copernican Space Science Center is at New Britain. The second-biggest telescope for public use in the United States is there. Visitors can look through it to study the stars.

Casting footprints at Dinosaur State Park

THE WESTERN INTERIOR

Bristol is west of New Britain. The American Clock & Watch Museum is there. Many of the clocks were

The old clock-repair shop at the American Clock & Watch Museum, in Bristol

Bristol and Terryville were once clock-making centers. Terryville also was a lock-making center.

made by Eli Terry. The hickory-dickory-dock clock has a toy mouse on it, as in the nursery rhyme. The New England Carousel Museum is also in Bristol. The museum has more than 300 merry-go-round horses and other figures.

West of Bristol is Terryville. The Lock Museum of America is there. About 22,000 locks and keys are on display. The oldest lock in the museum came from ancient Egypt. It is 4,000 years old.

Waterbury is south of Terryville. About 109,000 people live there. Waterbury is the state's fourth-biggest city. Millions of watches, clocks, and buttons have been made there. Waterbury's Mattatuck Museum has paintings by Connecticut artists. It also shows what Connecticut homes were like since the 1600s.

Danbury is southwest of Waterbury. It once led the country at making hats. The Scott-Fanton Museum has a replica of a 1790 Danbury hat shop.

To the north is Washington. The American Indian Archaeological Institute is there. Visitors view American Indian tools and artwork. Some are 10,000 years old. The institute also has a rebuilt Indian village of the 1600s.

Farther north is Litchfield. In 1774, America's first law school opened there. It was called Tapping

Reeve Law School. Today, visitors can tour the white cottage where the school was located.

Sharon is a good place to end a Connecticut tour. This town is in the Taconic Mountains in northwest Connecticut. Many of its homes were built during the Revolutionary War. Nearby is the Audubon Center. Trails lead through woods and fields of wildflowers. Turtles, owls, and other animals may be seen there.

Tapping Reeve House, site of the country's first law school

Overleaf: Harriet Beecher Stowe

45

A Gallery of Famous
Connecticut
People

A GALLERY OF FAMOUS CONNECTICUT PEOPLE

Nathan Hale

John Trumbull

Many famous people have come from Connecticut. They include authors, actresses, and scientists.

Benedict Arnold (1741-1801) was born in Norwich. He was an American general during the Revolutionary War. But in 1780, he turned traitor. For a large sum of money, he joined the British side. He led British forces at New London and Groton. Today, a disloyal person is often called a "Benedict Arnold."

Nathan Hale (1755-1776) was born in Coventry. Hale was a fine student and athlete at Yale. He played football and set a broad-jump record. Hale became a teacher (1773-1775). When the Revolutionary War began, he joined the army. Hale worked as a spy for George Washington. He was captured by the British. Before they hanged him, Hale said: "I only regret that I have but one life to lose for my country."

John Trumbull (1765-1843) was born in Lebanon. "Brother Jonathan" and Faith Trumbull were his parents. John became one of the country's early artists. He was well known for his paintings of

P.T. Barnum (seated, center) and his family

Lyman Beecher was born in New Haven; Catharine, in New York; and Harriet, in Litchfield.

Revolutionary War scenes. *The Signing of the Declaration of Independence* is his best-known work.

Noah Webster (1758-1843) was born in West Hartford. He became a teacher. In Webster's time, a word could be spelled several ways. Webster thought there should be one correct way to spell each word. In 1783, *Webster's American Spelling Book* came out. Over many years, about 60 million copies were sold. Webster then wrote the first dictionary in the United States. It was called *An American Dictionary of the English Language.*

Lyman Beecher (1775-1863) was a minister who preached against slavery. **Catharine Beecher** (1800-1878) was the eldest of his thirteen children.

48

She founded girls' schools in Connecticut and Ohio. Catharine was also the first American to teach home economics classes. Lyman's daughter **Harriet Beecher Stowe** (1811-1896) wrote *Uncle Tom's Cabin.*

Phineas T. "P. T." Barnum (1810-1891) was born in Bethel. In 1841, he opened Barnum's American Museum in New York. There, he first showed General Tom Thumb. In 1871, he founded "The Greatest Show on Earth." It was a circus and traveling museum. The show included a fake mermaid and Jumbo, a huge elephant. Barnum was also a politician. He served in Connecticut's legislature. He was also mayor of Bridgeport.

Frederick Law Olmsted (1822-1903) was born in Hartford. Olmsted became a landscape architect. He drew up plans for about eighty parks. One big project was New York City's Central Park. Another was the Capitol grounds in Washington, D.C.

Barbara McClintock (1902-1992) was born in Hartford. As a teenager, she grew to love science. McClintock became a geneticist. She studied how parents pass traits to their children. Her work has helped doctors use medicines to fight infections. Plant experts also use her methods. They have bred

Frederick Law Olmsted

Barbara McClintock

better crops to feed the world. In 1983, she won the Nobel Prize in medicine.

Benjamin Spock was born in New Haven in 1903. He attended Yale University. In 1924, Spock was on the U.S. rowing team. The team won an Olympic gold medal. Later, Spock became a children's doctor. He wrote *Baby and Child Care*. This book helps parents raise their children. It has sold more than 40 million copies in twenty-five languages.

Eleanor Estes (1906-1988) was also born in New Haven. She wrote her first story at the age of

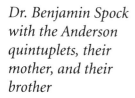

Dr. Benjamin Spock with the Anderson quintuplets, their mother, and their brother

eleven. Estes's first book was *The Moffats*. It was published in 1941. The book is about a small-town New England family. Her book *Ginger Pye* won the 1952 Newbery Medal.

Al Capp (1909-1979) was born in New Haven. He grew up in Bridgeport. As a boy, Capp drew his own comic strips. He sold them to neighbor children. Capp later created "Li'l Abner." This famous comic strip appeared in many newspapers. It was about the Yokums. They were a mountain family in a place called Dogpatch. Capp used "Li'l Abner" to poke fun at famous people.

Katharine Hepburn was born in Hartford in 1909. At first, she wanted to be a doctor like her father. But she decided to become an actress instead. Her films included *Little Women, Bringing Up Baby, and The African Queen*. Hepburn is the only movie star to win four best actress awards.

Ella T. Grasso (1919-1981) was born in Windsor Locks. Grasso became one of the most popular lawmakers in Connecticut. In twenty-six years, she never lost an election. From 1975 to 1980, Grasso was Connecticut's governor. She was the first woman governor in the United States elected on her own. Others had followed their husbands in the office. Grasso became ill during her second

Katharine Hepburn

Ella Grasso

Dorothy Hamill

term. She ran the state from her hospital bed. After she died, Connecticuters placed THANK YOU, ELLA stickers on their cars.

Lowell P. Weicker, Jr., was born in France in 1931. He served Connecticut in the U.S. House of Representatives (1969-1971). Then, he was in the U.S. Senate (1971-1989). He worked on behalf of health care and disabled people. Weicker was elected Connecticut's governor in 1990. The state's first income tax was passed in 1991, a very unpopular decision for the voters.

Ralph Nader was born in Winsted in 1934. He wrote *Unsafe at Any Speed*. That book helped get laws passed for car seat belts and air bags. Nader has also worked to improve American food products and health care.

Terry Backer was born in Stamford in 1954. He comes from a family of fishermen. Backer catches oysters in Long Island Sound. During the mid-1980s, the sound was very polluted. In 1987, Backer started patrolling the sound to stop polluters. In 1992, he was elected to the state legislature.

Dorothy Hamill was born in Riverside in 1956. At the age of eight, she received ice skates for Christmas. Hamill became a great skater. At the

1976 Winter Olympics, she won a gold medal for figure skating.

Birthplace of Ella Grasso, P. T. Barnum, Barbara McClintock, and Nathan Hale . . .

Home also to Katharine Hepburn, "Brother Jonathan" Trumbull, Eleanor Estes, and Benjamin Spock . . .

The state known for the Fundamental Orders, the Charter Oak, and the USS *Nautilus* . . .

Today, the site of the U.S. Coast Guard Academy and a center for the insurance industry . . .

This is the Constitution State—Connecticut!

Did You Know?

The country's first children's magazine was published at Hartford in 1789. It was called *The Children's Magazine.*

William Gray of Hartford invented the baseball chest protector for catchers in 1878. In 1889, Gray also invented the coin-operated telephone.

Connecticut has towns named Hampton and East Hampton. But East Hampton is west of Hampton.

Thomas H. Gallaudet and Laurent Clerc founded the country's first school for the deaf at Hartford in 1817. Called the American School for the Deaf, it is now at West Hartford.

The Podunk Indians' village was near present-day Hartford. Their name inspired the word *podunk,* which means a very small town.

Connecticut had strict laws during the 1700s. It was a crime to play sports, sail, or even laugh on Sunday.

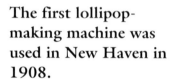

The first lollipop-making machine was used in New Haven in 1908.

Three Connecticut teams have won the Little League World Series in Pennsylvania. Stamford won in 1951, Windsor Locks in 1965, and Trumbull in 1989. The Trumbull team beat heavily favored Taiwan 5-2.

David Bushnell of Saybrook built the first American submarine, the *Turtle,* during the Revolutionary War.

Millions of people love Wiffle Ball. This is a baseball game in which a plastic ball and bat are used. David Mullany of Fairfield invented Wiffle Ball in 1953 for his thirteen-year-old son. That year, Mullany began the Wiffle Ball Company, now in Shelton.

The country's first children's library was begun at Salisbury in 1803. The first U.S. bicycle factory was established at Hartford in 1877. The country's first telephone book was issued at New Haven in 1878.

When she was only fourteen, Dorothy Hamill invented an ice-skating spin called the "Hamill camel."

Patents grant people rights to their inventions. In 1809, South Killingly inventor Mary Kies became the first woman granted a U.S. patent. It was for a weaving machine.

P. T. Barnum's circus featured a 15,000-pound elephant named Jumbo. Jumbo's name came to mean extra-big, as in jumbo jet.

P.T. BARNUM'S GREATEST SHOW ON EARTH. & THE GREAT LONDON CIRCUS COMBINED WITH
THE GIANT AFRICAN ELEPHANT
JUMBO
JUMBO COOLED
JUMBO ON HIS TRAVELS
THE REMOVAL OF THE BIGGEST ELEPHANT IN THE WORLD. WAS REMONSTRATED AGAINST BY THE WHOLE BRITISH NATION.
SANGER'S ROYAL BRITISH MENAGERIE & GRAND INTERNATIONAL ALLIED SHOWS.
BARNUM, BAILEY & HUTCHINSON, SOLE OWNERS.

In 1937, Connecticut became the first state to issue permanent license plates for cars.

CONNECTICUT INFORMATION

State flag

Praying mantis

Garnets

Area: 5,018 square miles (only two states are smaller)

Greatest Distance North to South: 75 miles

Greatest Distance East to West: 90 miles

Borders: Rhode Island to the east; Massachusetts to the north; New York to the west; Long Island Sound to the south

Highest Point: 2,380 feet above sea level, on Connecticut's part of Mount Frissell

Lowest Point: Sea level, along Long Island Sound

Hottest Recorded Temperature: 106° F. (at Danbury, on July 15, 1995)

Coldest Recorded Temperature: -32° F. (at Falls Village, on February 16, 1943)

Statehood: The fifth state, on January 9, 1788

Origin of Name: From the Indian word *quinnehtukqut,* which means "beside the long river." In English, it became *Connecticut*

Capital: Hartford

Counties: 8

United States Senators: 2

United States Representatives: 6 (as of 1992)

State Senators: 36

State Representatives: 151

State Song: "Yankee Doodle," composer unknown

State Motto: *Qui transtulit sustinet* (Latin for "He who transplanted still sustains," which means "The Lord who sent us here still watches over us")

Nicknames: Constitution State, Land of Steady Habits, Provisions State, Nutmeg State

State Seal: Established in 1784

State Flag: Adopted in 1897

State Flower: Mountain laurel

State Bird: Robin

State Tree: White oak

State Hero: Nathan Hale

State Insect: Praying mantis

State Animal: Sperm whale

State Mineral: Garnet

State Shellfish: Eastern oyster

State Ship: USS *Nautilus*

Mountain laurel

State Fossil: *Eubrontes giganteus* (dinosaur tracks)

Some Rivers: Connecticut, Housatonic, Naugatuck, Shepaug, Quinnipiac, Shetucket, Willimantic, Quinebaug, Thames

Lakes and Ponds: Lake Candlewood, Bantam, Shenipsit, Twin Lakes, Waramaug

Wildlife: White-tailed deer, beavers, river otters, muskrats, coyotes, opossums, red foxes, raccoons, minks, rabbits, robins, woodpeckers, ring-necked pheasants, ducks, swans, great blue herons, many other kinds of birds, lobsters, oysters, clams, bass, perch, trout, mackerel, swordfish, cod, flounder, many other kinds of fish

Farm Products: Flowers, shrubs, many other greenhouse and nursery plants, eggs, milk, apples, pears, beef, hay, mushrooms, tobacco

Manufactured Products: Helicopters, submarines, jet engines, and other transportation equipment, medical instruments, computers and other machinery, watches and clocks, nuts and bolts, many other kinds of hardware and metal products, pens and pencils, chemicals, toys, bakery products and other foods

Mining Products: Crushed stone, sand and gravel, clays

Population: 3,287,116, twenty-seventh among the states (1990 U.S. Census Bureau figures)

Major Cities (1990 Census):

Bridgeport	141,686	Norwalk	78,331
Hartford	139,739	New Britain	75,491
New Haven	130,474	Danbury	65,585
Waterbury	108,961	Bristol	60,640
Stamford	106,056	West Hartford	60,110

Robin

White Oak

CONNECTICUT HISTORY

Fife and Drum marchers on Memorial Day in Waterbury

8000 B.C.—Prehistoric Indians reach Connecticut

1614—Dutch explorer Adriaen Block becomes the first known European in Connecticut

1633—The Dutch build a trading post at present-day Hartford; the English found Windsor, their first Connecticut town

1636—The towns of Hartford, Wethersfield, and Windsor form the Connecticut Colony

1636-37—The colonists defeat the Pequots in the Pequot War

1638—The New Haven Colony is founded

1639—The Fundamental Orders, the first written constitution in the Americas, is approved

1662—The king of England grants a charter to the Connecticut Colony

1665—The New Haven Colony joins the Connecticut Colony

1687—The colonists hide the charter in the Charter Oak

1702—Yale University opens

1737—Samuel Higley of Simsbury mints the first American copper coins

1764—The *Connecticut Courant,* today called the *Hartford Courant* and the country's oldest continuous newspaper, is begun

1775-83—The colonists win their freedom from England in the Revolutionary War

1776—Nathan Hale is hanged as a spy by the British

1787—The Connecticut Compromise helps work out the U.S. Constitution

1788—On January 9, Connecticut becomes the fifth state

1793—Eli Whitney invents the cotton gin

1806—Noah Webster publishes the first English dictionary in the United States

1848—The last slaves in Connecticut are freed

1861—The Civil War begins

1863—The first accident insurance company in the United States is begun at Hartford

1865—The North wins the Civil War and the South's slaves are freed; more than 20,000 of over 57,000 Connecticut troops die in the war

1881—The University of Connecticut is founded

1888—Happy 100th birthday, Constitution State!

1898—The first automobile insurance in the United States is issued at Hartford

1917-18—Nearly 70,000 Connecticuters help win World War I

1929-39—The Great Depression causes massive joblessness in Connecticut and the rest of the country

1941-45—After the United States enters World War II, about 233,000 Connecticut men and women help win the war

1954—The *Nautilus,* the first nuclear submarine, is launched at Groton

1965—The present state constitution is adopted

1974—Ella Grasso is the first woman in the United States elected in her own right as a state governor

1981—Thirman Milner is elected mayor of Hartford, becoming the first black mayor of a New England city

1987—Carrie Saxon Perry is elected mayor of Hartford, becoming the first black woman elected mayor of a large U.S. city

1988—Happy 200th birthday, Constitution State!

1991—Lowell P. Weicker, Jr., becomes governor; Connecticut adopts a state income tax

1994—John Rowland becomes governor

1995—The University of Connecticut Huskies win the NCAA women's basketball championship

A Connecticut Union soldier

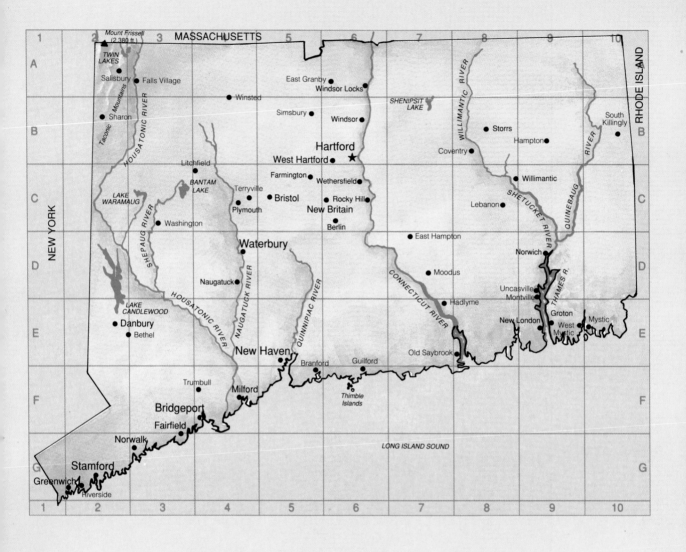

MAP KEY

GLOSSARY

ancient: Relating to a time early in history

billion: A thousand million (1,000,000,000)

capital: A city that is the seat of government

capitol: A building in which the government meets

climate: The typical weather of a region

coast: The land along a large body of water

colony: A settlement that is outside a parent country and that is ruled by the parent country

compromise: An agreement in which both sides give in on some points

constitution: A framework of government, or a set of basic laws

depression: A period of very hard times with widespread joblessness

explorer: A person who visits and studies unknown lands

fundamental: Basic

geneticist: A scientist who studies how parents pass traits to their children

glacier: A mass of slowly moving ice

hurricane: A huge storm that forms over an ocean

industry: A business activity that needs many people to produce goods or services

inventor: A person who develops a new machine or a new way of doing something

landscape architect: A person who plans parks and other lands for human use

legislature: A lawmaking body

manufacturing: The making of products

million: A thousand thousand (1,000,000)

population: The number of people in a place

provisions: Supplies

slavery: A practice in which some people are owned by other people

This covered bridge at West Cornwall was built in 1837.

PICTURE ACKNOWLEDGMENTS

Front cover, © Michael Giannaccio/**N E Stock Photo**; 1, © Leonard Hellerman/**N E Stock Photo**; 2, **Tom Dunnington**; 3, © Jackie Linder/**N E Stock Photo**; 4-5, **Tom Dunnington**; 6-7, © **Tom Till**; 8, © **Tom Till**; 9 (left), © **David Forbert**; 9 (right), **Courtesy of Hammond Incorporated, Maplewood, New Jersey**; 10 (top), © Wendy Shatil/Bob Rozinski/**Tom Stack & Associates**; 10 (bottom), © C. Postmus/**Root Resources**; 11, © H. Schmeiser/**N E Stock Photo**; 12, **Copyrighted by the White House Historical Association; photograph by the National Geographic Society**; 13, © Michael Giannaccio/**N E Stock Photo**; 15, **Stock Montage, Inc.**; 16, **Courtesy of Connecticut Historical Society**; 17, **Courtesy of Connecticut Historical Society**; 18, © Vernon Sigl/**SuperStock**; 19, **Courtesy of Connecticut Historical Society**; 20, **Courtesy of Connecticut Historical Society**; 21, **Stock Montage, Inc.**; 22 (top), **Stock Montage, Inc.**; 22 (bottom), © **1993 Stock Montage, Inc.**; 23, **North Wind Picture Archives**; 24, **Courtesy of Connecticut Historical Society**; 25, **Courtesy of Connecticut Historical Society**; 26, **AP/Wide World Photos**; 27, © Michael Giannaccio/**N E Stock Photo**; 28, © Lou Palmieri/**N E Stock Photo**; 29 (top), © **Joseph A. DiChello, Jr.**; 29 (bottom), © **Mary Ann Brockman**; 30 (left), © Chuck Schmeiser/**N E Stock Photo**; 30 (right), © **Joseph A. DiChello, Jr.**; 31, © **Joseph A. DiChello, Jr.**; 32-33, © Tom Algire/**SuperStock**; 34, © Fred George/**Tony Stone Images, Inc.**; 35 (top), © **David Forbert**; 35 (bottom), © Michael Giannaccio/**N E Stock Photo**; 36 (top), © Michael Giannaccio/**N E Stock Photo**; 36 (bottom), © The Photo Source/**SuperStock**; 37, © **Joseph A. DiChello, Jr.**; 38, © **Photri**; 39, © Leonard Friend/**N E Stock Photo**; 40, © **Photri**; 41, © **Gene Ahrens**; 42 (top), © **Joseph A. DiChello, Jr.**; 42 (bottom), © Michael Giannaccio/**N E Stock Photo**; 43 (top), © **Mary Ann Brockman**; 43 (bottom), © Fred M. Dole/**N E Stock Photo**; 44, © Michael Giannaccio/**N E Stock Photo**; 45, © David Forbert/**SuperStock**; 46, **Sophie Smith Collection, Smith College, Northampton, MA**; 47 (top), **Courtesy of Connecticut Historical Society**; 47 (bottom), **Dictionary of American Portraits**; 48, **National Portrait Gallery, Smithsonian Institution/Art Resource, NY**; 49 (both pictures), **AP/Wide World Photos**; 50, **AP/Wide World Photos**; 51 (top), **AP/Wide World Photos**; 51 (bottom), **Connecticut State Library**; 52, **AP/Wide World Photos**; 53, **Wide World Photos, Inc.**; 54, **Courtesy National Museum of American History/Southern New England Telephone**; 54-55, © John David Harper/**N E Stock Photo**; 55, **Reproduced by permission of Ringling Bros.-Barnum & Bailey Combined Shows, Inc., from the collection of Circus World Museum, Baraboo, Wisconsin**; 56 (top), **Courtesy Flag Research Center, Winchester, Massachusetts 01890**; 56 (middle), © Earl L. Kubis/**Root Resources**; 56 (bottom), © Mary A. Root/**Root Resources**; 57 (top), © Fred M. Dole/**N E Stock Photo**; 57 (middle), © **James P. Rowan**; 57 (bottom), © Ruth Smith/**Root Resources**; 58, © **Photri**; 59, **Courtesy of Connecticut Historical Society**; 60, **Tom Dunnington**; 62, © **Tom Till**; back cover, © **David Forbert**

INDEX

Page numbers in boldface type indicate illustrations.

ABOUT THE AUTHORS

Dennis and Judith Fradin have coauthored several books in the From Sea to Shining Sea series. The Fradins both graduated from Northwestern University in 1967. Dennis has been a professional writer for twenty years, and has published 150 books. His works for Childrens Press include the Young People's Stories of Our States series, the Disaster! series, and the Thirteen Colonies series. Judith earned her M.A. in literature from Northwestern University and taught high-school and college English for many years. The Fradins, who are the parents of Anthony, Diana, and Michael, live in Evanston, Illinois.